AF269772

POISON DART Frogs

by Aubrey Zalewski

Content Consultant

Ralph A. Saporito, PhD
Associate Professor
Department of Biology
John Carroll University

CAPSTONE PRESS
a capstone imprint

Bright Idea Books are published by Capstone Press
1710 Roe Crest Drive, North Mankato, Minnesota 56003
www.mycapstone.com

Library of Congress Cataloging-in-Publication Data
Names: Zalewski, Aubrey, author.
Title: Poison dart frogs / by Aubrey Zalewski.
Description: North Mankato, Minnesota : Capstone Press, [2020] | Series:
   Unique animal adaptations | Includes bibliographical references and index. |
   Audience: Grade 4 to 6. |
Identifiers: LCCN 2019003132 (print) | LCCN 2019004108 (ebook) | ISBN
   9781543571783 (ebook) | ISBN 9781543571646 (hardcover) | ISBN
   9781543575125 (paperback)
Subjects: LCSH: Dendrobatidae--Juvenile literature.
Classification: LCC QL668.E233 (ebook) | LCC QL668.E233 Z35 2020 (print) |
   DDC 597.8/77--dc23
LC record available at https://lccn.loc.gov/2019003132

All internet sites appearing in back matter were available and accurate when this book was sent to press.

Editorial Credits
Editor: Marie Pearson
Designer: Becky Daum
Production Specialist: Colleen McLaren

Photo Credits
Alamy: F. Rauschenbach/F1online digitale Bildagentur GmbH, 6–7; iStockphoto: Freder, 13; Shutterstock Images: Bos11, 16–17, Chris Alcock, 19, Christian Vinces, 26, Dirk Ercken, cover (top), cover (bottom), 5, 8–9, 11, 14–15, 20, 25, 28, 31, Dr Morley Read, 23, mspoli, cover (background)

Design Elements: Shutterstock Images

TABLE OF CONTENTS

CHAPTER 1

TINY BUT
Dangerous

A frog hops on the rain forest floor. It is the size of a paper clip. But it is easy to see. It has bright colors. It is a poison dart frog. Poison dart frogs are the brightest colored frogs in the world. They can be red, yellow, green, blue, gold, and black. But watch out! These frogs are very **poisonous**. They are among the most poisonous animals in the world.

MANY COLORS

The harlequin poison frog can be more than 30 different colors.

There are more than 100 **species** of poison dart frogs. They are found in Central and South America. This part of the world is full of rain forests. Many of the frogs live on the rain forest floor. They eat ants, mites, and beetles.

A poison dart frog
uses its tongue to
catch prey.

For many years, people have used poison dart frogs for darts. That is how the frogs got their name. People in Colombia used darts for hunting. The people would rub darts on the frogs' backs. The poison could kill a large monkey.

The brighter a frog's colors, the more poisonous it might be.

CHAPTER 2

ADAPTING TO Survive

The rain forest is dangerous. Many animals hide. But poison dart frogs do not. Some stand out with bright colors. These colors are an **adaptation**. They warn **predators** that the frog is poisonous. Predators know not to eat the frog.

Bright colors warn
other animals to
stay away.

Some frogs use their colors as **camouflage**. Blue and yellow colors can look bright up close. From a distance, the colors blend in with the forest plants.

Poison dart frogs get their poison from their food. The frogs eat poisonous bugs. The poison builds up in the frogs' bodies. This poison does not hurt the frogs. Their bodies have adapted.

A frog's colors
can help keep
it safe in the
rain forest.

The golden poison frog is the most poisonous. Its poison can kill a human. The poison makes a heart stop. Other frogs are not as toxic. But they can make predators sick.

NOT ALWAYS POISONOUS

Some poison dart frogs live in **captivity**. These frogs do not eat poisonous bugs. The frogs are not poisonous.

Golden poison frogs live in Colombia in South America.

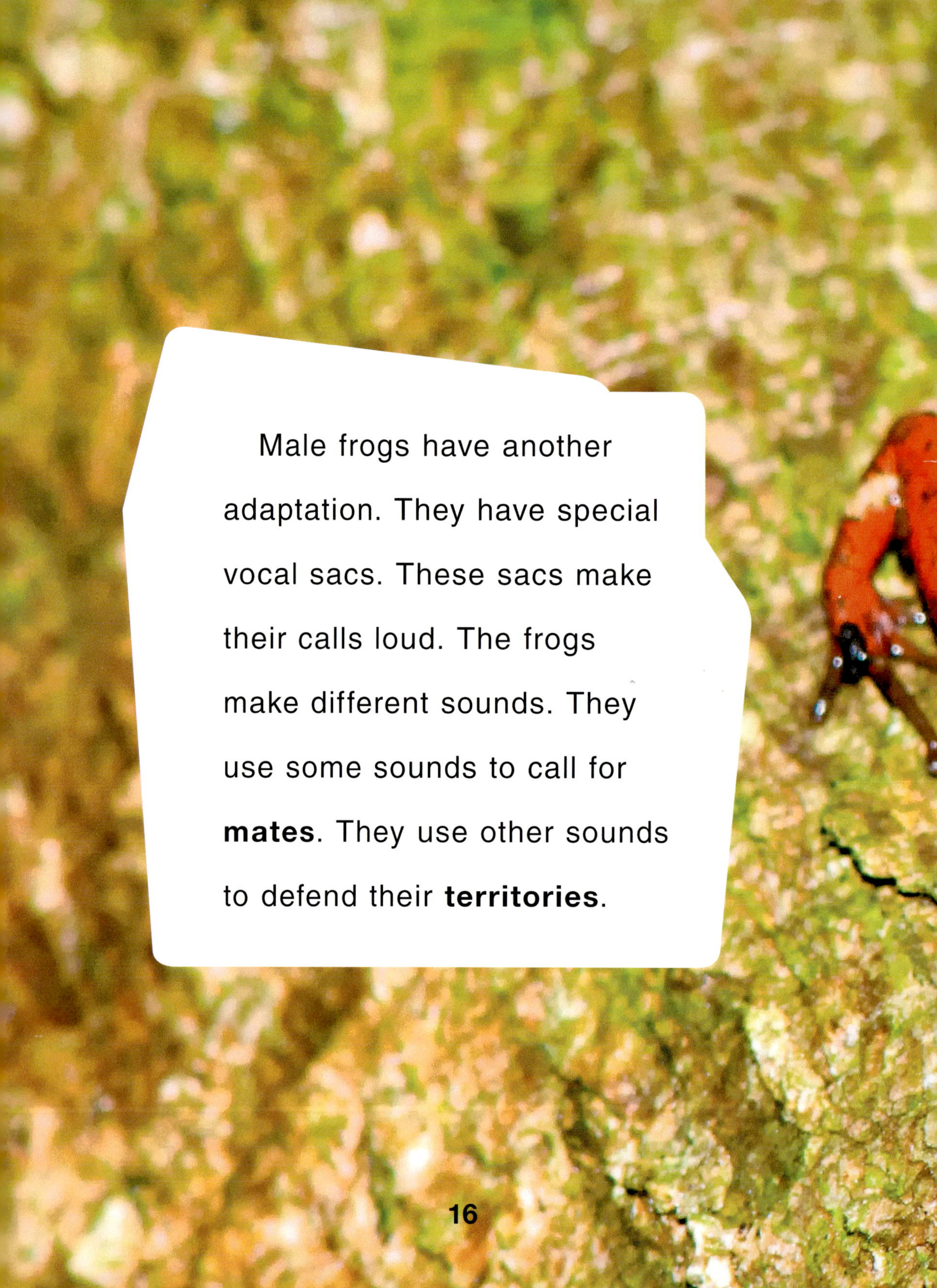

Male frogs have another adaptation. They have special vocal sacs. These sacs make their calls loud. The frogs make different sounds. They use some sounds to call for **mates**. They use other sounds to defend their **territories**.

The vocal sac expands
when the frog calls.

LIFE Cycle

A male poison dart frog calls a female. They mate. They decide where to lay the eggs. The eggs need a dark and moist place. The female lays the eggs inside fallen leaves. Some frogs lay their eggs in plants. Males guard the eggs. They keep the eggs from drying out. Sometimes females help too.

Poison dart frogs may
lay their eggs on leaves.

Tadpoles hatch from the eggs. They don't have legs yet. They have long tails. They need water. The parents carry them on their backs. They take the tadpoles to small pools of water. Sometimes they carry many.

The tadpoles stay in the water for about six to eight weeks. The time depends on the species. They grow legs. Their tails get shorter. They become **juveniles**. They do not need the water anymore. The frogs can live for 3 to 15 years.

EGG DINNER

Some poison dart frogs lay eggs for the tadpoles to eat.

CHAPTER 4

PROTECTING Poison Dart Frogs

Many poison dart frogs are **endangered**. People cut down rain forests. This takes away the frogs' **habitat**.

Poison dart frogs
cannot survive without
their rain forest habitat.

23

People take the frogs from
the wild. They sell them illegally.
Many frogs do not survive.
Those that are left behind do
not do well either. There are
fewer frogs in the wild. They
have a hard time finding mates.

Poison dart frogs
are popular for their
bright colors.

Poison dart frogs are important. They control the number of insects in the rain forest. They can also help science. Scientists study the frogs' poison. They want to use it to make medicine.

People are working to save these frogs. They breed the frogs. One day, they hope to put those frogs back in the wild.

A DEADLY DISEASE

The chytrid fungus is dangerous for frogs. It grows in the frogs' habitat. It attacks the frogs' skin. About 200 amphibian species have gone **extinct** because of it.

GLOSSARY

adaptation
a behavior or body part that helps an animal survive in its environment

camouflage
a color pattern that blends in with the surroundings

captivity
the condition of being kept or trapped by people

endangered
when a species is in danger of going extinct

extinct
died out, with no more living members

habitat
the place where a living thing lives

juvenile
no longer a baby but not yet an adult

mate
the male or female partners of animals

poisonous
harmful or deadly when taken into the body

predator
an animal that eats other animals

species
a group of animals that are the same; these animals can mate and have offspring

territory
an area that an animal lives in and defends

1. Poison dart frogs are diurnal. That means that they are active during the day. Most tropical frogs are active at night.

2. Some poison dart frogs carry their tadpoles to bromeliads. These are tropical flowering plants. Bromeliads collect rainwater. They have small pools for the tadpoles to swim in.

3. Some tadpoles are poisonous too. They get their poison from their mothers.

4. Poison dart frogs are also called poison arrow frogs.

ACTIVITY

SAVE THE FROGS

People use education to help save poison dart frogs. They teach others not to buy illegal pets. They also teach them about saving the rain forest. If people know about the frogs, they will want to help them. Make a booklet about poison dart frogs. Include facts about the poison dart frog. Research ways that you and others can help save the frogs. Put those tips in the booklet. Decorate it so it looks nice. You can use this booklet to teach others about saving poison dart frogs.

FURTHER RESOURCES

**Want to learn more about poison dart frogs?
Visit these websites:**

National Geographic Kids: Poison Dart Frog
https://kids.nationalgeographic.com/animals/poison-dart-frog/#poison-dart-
   frog-orange-blue.jpg

San Diego Zoo Kids: Poison Frog
https://kids.sandiegozoo.org/animals/poison-frog

**Want to learn about other amphibians?
Check out these sources:**

Guillain, Charlotte. *Life Story of a Salamander*. Animal Life Stories. Chicago:
   Heinemann-Raintree, 2015.

National Geographic Kids: Amphibians
https://kids.nationalgeographic.com/animals/hubs/amphibians/

Royston, Angela. *Amphibians*. Animal Classifications. Chicago:
   Heinemann-Raintree, 2015.

INDEX